Sojourners

of the

In–Between

Books by Gregory Djanikian

Dear Gravity
So I Will Till the Ground
Years Later
About Distance
Falling Deeply into America
The Man in the Middle

Sojourners
of the
In-Between

Gregory Djanikian

Carnegie Mellon University Press
Pittsburgh 2020

Acknowledgments

Thank you to the editors of the following journals in which some of these poems first appeared:

The Adroit Journal: "All Those Whom I Have Loved," "Even During the Slightest Changes," "Episode at the Neighbor's House"
The Atlanta Review: "My Mother Considers Her Death During Cocktail Hour," "A Roost of Turkeys," "Bats"
Boulevard: "Harbingers"
Cimarron Review: "During Our Conversation I'd Like To Interrupt To Say"
Cleaver Magazine: "Beauty," "What I Was Thinking of During the Funeral Service, Douglas, Arizona"
The Cortland Review: "Inside Man"
crazyhorse: "Music Making," "When It Is Time," "A Moment Without Objects"
The Florida Review: "No Comment"
Hampden-Sydney Poetry Review: "Undoing Song," "Just the Facts"
Juxtaprose: "My 90-Year-Old Mother Would Be an Alpinist"
The New Criterion: "Lies"
New Ohio Review: "Banality," "And Another Thing," "Loose Ends"
Nimrod: "Homecoming"
Poet Lore: "Traveling into Deeper Country"
Poetry Northwest: "What We Don't Know Won't Kill Us, Or It Will," "Reconstitutions, Dispersions"
Smartish Pace: "An Uneven Dozen"
Solstice: "Body to Body," "Horse Heaven"
Tampa Review: "Sometimes," "Ghost Dog"
Tar River Poetry: "Other Lessons"

"Lies" and "A Roost of Turkeys" appeared on *Poetry Daily*
"Harbingers" and "Banality" appeared on *Verse Daily*

Many thanks to Alysa Bennett, Ariel Djanikian, and Philip Sandick for their suggestions and critical help. Thanks also to those at Carnegie Mellon University Press, Gerald Costanzo, Cynthia Lamb, and Connie Amoroso for bringing this collection together.

Book design by Connie Amoroso

Library of Congress Control Number 2019953774
ISBN 978-0-88748-652-4
Copyright © 2020 by Gregory Djanikian
All rights reserved
Printed and bound in the United States of America

10 9 8 7 6 5 4 3 2 1

for Stephen Dunn and Al Filreis
who have made a difference

Contents

I   Harbingers / 13
What We Don't Know Won't Kill Us, Or It Will / 15
Inside Man / 17
Music Making / 18
Banality / 20
No Comment / 22
My 90-Year-Old Mother Would Be an Alpinist / 23
What Is a Cat But a Voice Among All the Other Voices / 25

II   Surprises / 29
During Our Conversation I'd Like To Interrupt To Say / 31
Poem with Clouds / 33
And Another Thing / 35
Let's Put an End to Grace / 37
Nostalgia / 39
Loose Ends / 41
Lies / 42

III   Sometimes / 47
Bats / 48
Beauty / 49
Body to Body / 50
Startled from Sleep / 51
Undoing Song / 52
When It Is Time / 53
Homecoming / 54
Stuff / 55
All Those Whom I Have Loved / 57
Other Lessons / 58

IV   A Moment Without Objects / 61
Even During the Slightest Changes / 62
Episode at the Neighbor's House / 63
What I Was Thinking of During the Funeral Service,
       Douglas, Arizona / 64
Just the Facts / 65
Change / 66
Why I'm Not in Cairo (Care-O), Illinois, Honking
       My Horn Like a Happy Tourist / 68
Traveling into Deeper Country / 69

V   My Mother Considers Her Death During Cocktail Hour / 75
Ghost Dog / 77
Horse Heaven / 78
A Roost of Turkeys / 80
An Uneven Dozen / 81
Reconstitutions, Dispersions / 85
Bad News Day in Spring / 86
What I Want / 88
Thankfulness / 89

A tree cannot grow in the sky, nor clouds be in the deep sea,
nor fish live in the fields, nor can blood be in sticks,
nor sap in the rocks.

—Lucretius, *On the Nature of Things*

I like to find
what's not found
at once, but lies
within something of another nature
in repose, distinct.

—Denise Levertov, "Pleasures"

I

Harbingers

Always the small before the large,
the early crocus before the full-bloomed garden,
the single firefly until the thousand lights.

That man in the pink Hawaiian shirt
and those clunky snowmobile boots—
I don't know why he seems so lost
standing on the sidewalk in Hardwick, VT,
but yes, I would like to say to him
thank you for making an appearance,
and more brilliance please.

It's like the priest who walks into a bar
with a frozen mackerel under his arm
yelling *Fish, sure, I give you fish!*
while every astonished eye waits
for the loaves to appear, and maybe the wine.

Sometimes the earth's a desert of promise,
the world-soul damaged, dream-cities ruined.
Other times you wish to keep living in it
to see the parade by your door.

For instance, just this morning
one robin, then a hundred in the yard
pecking at the grass for seeds,
fat city for a thing with feathers.

And here's the street corner mime
ventriloquizing through a dummy
who also seems to be a mime!—
but isn't there a place for it,
the unheard words making us suddenly think
of the many that might be spoken?

Haven't we imagined the end of the drought
by feeling one droplet of rain?
Or wanted to paint the whole town red
by seeing a sun-streak at dusk?

I mean, here's a pot of gold:
don't we always look for the rainbow
to travel back to where everything started?

What We Don't Know Won't Kill Us,
Or It Will

Of course, there's Yellowstone, that massive, steamy, volcanic
churning underneath all the buffalo and bear
and the tourist cars lined up like tin cans.

Meanwhile, the asteroids are whizzing by
like warheads, missile-driven, nuclear,
arcing over our tiny wooden desks.
And here's an airplane coming in for a landing, or not.

Down the street, someone is mowing his lawn
and cursing the clover and crabgrass,
and another trimming her rosebush
whose leaves are already, pockmarked, lacy,
the beetles glistening like onyx.

I've never said to anyone, "Look up,"
or "put your ear next to the ground,
it might change your life."
Except to myself a hundred times,
but I keep forgetting.

And here I am waxing my car
just to see my reflection in the hood
floating above a vast array of pistons, belts,
combustive power I have no notion of.

Whatever has a surface has a deeper meaning.
This table. These chairs. This floor
that holds me up without my asking.

Today, I saw a man set up a canvas on his easel
next to a faded barn, begin to paint the sky
before anything else, and a quarter mile away,
a woman was visiting a gravesite, laying flowers

in the cut grass, both of them clearing a space
so they could add to it, making what they wanted.

I don't want to know everything,
no purpose or fun in it, or puzzle.
Sometimes the future is a deep blur
from which we emerge, trailing clouds
not so much of glory but appetite.

Here's to the future.
I'm washing the tablecloth from last night's party
and the wine bottles are clinking like bells,
ring in the new.

Whatever happens, we are here to say
it happened. At least up until.
Which seems enough time
to think about it.

Inside Man

My father was an inside man,
hotel room smoke-
loving casino man.

Loved nothing of the rose
or walking stick, nothing
of beebalm or the bee.

The sound of the rain falling
was the sound of my father
wanting to come in.

The sound of the wind bending the trees
was my father thinking *asphalt*,
roadbed, every possible hardness.

His heaviest coat in any weather.
The shortest cuts to every drive
without grass or gardenias.

Now I think my cat curling into a box
must be my father, my dog disappearing
under the bed must be his likeness.

I throw my arms out,
I sweep away closets, cocoons,
crack the oyster open.

My father loved the sound of chips
falling from one hand into another,
the gurgle of liquor over ice.

"I'm an inside man," he'd say
wherever he was, adjusting his body
to fit the dark, the light, the in-between.

Music Making

The bells are ringing in their towers,
the acorns are dangling by a thread
from the wind-tossed trees.

Last night coyotes were yipping
to each other across the valley,
and this morning, the raucous birds repeated
the story in their own versions.

Sometimes I don't know
whether to applaud or
cover my ears. Or sing along.

The refrigerator has clicked and hummed
at odd hours of the night,
and now my cat is walking over my keyboard,
tapping out a blessing I wish I could understand.

The world's blips and pings, street traffic,
glass clatter, hammer clank, make up,
John Cage said once, maybe plunking a clothesline,
the irreproducible music of our lives.

And I'm adding to it without effort,
just one of millions in this musical drift,
shoes clacking against the sidewalk,
newspapers rustling mid-commute,
the office of twang and timbre open for business
and everyone invited.

Let a choir of angels join with their open mouths.
Let the devil stand among them
pitching his stones into a lake.

I've turned over a rock. Even the wood-lice
are scuttling in the dirt, making
as much noise as they can.

The world turns on a needle.
Everything I've said out loud
has bumped into something or other,

even as ephemeral as vapor or smoke,
causing such small riots of sound,
imperceptible changes of direction.

Banality

There's something to be said for banality,
the way it keeps everything on a level plane,
one cliché blithely following another
like cows heading toward the pasture.

How lovely sometimes not to think
about Russian Futurism, or the second law
of thermodynamics, or how thinking itself
requires some thoughtfulness.

I'd like to ask if Machiavelli
ever owned a dog named "Prince."
I'd like to imagine Rosalind Franklin
lounging pleasantly by a wood stove.

Let the mind take a holiday,
the body put its slippers on.
It's a beautiful day, says the banal,
and today, I'm happy to agree
with its genial locutions.

Woof, woof, goes the neighbor's dog.
The sun is pouring in through the window,
heating up the parlor, the blue sky is so blue,
and the cumulous clouds are looking very cumulous.

I'm all for reading a murder mystery,
something with flair but forgettable.
Or some novelette whose hero's name
is Hawk or Kestrel, a raptor bird
soaring above his ravished love.

I'm lying on the couch with easy puzzles.
I'm playing a song that has no accidentals.
Life's but a dream, comme ci, comme ça.

No doubt, tomorrow I'll be famished
for what's occult and perilous,
all those knots in the brain,
all the words that are hard to crack.

Today, I'm floating like a feather,
call me Falcon, look me up
in the field guide under Blissful,
Empty-headed, under everything
that loves what it does today,
and requires no explanation.

No Comment

Maybe I'd like someone to look at me
and say *No comment*, which might mean
something crucial has been left unsaid.

I wouldn't mind that kind of attention
like anyone who wants to be singled out
even by a crazy spotlight.

After all, aren't we relegated
to the slush pile when the time comes,
all those bleak grave gardens,
headstones with rubbed-out names?

Maybe it's why I cast my father's ashes
into the Atlantic near the casinos he loved,
the luck that could change one man
into another, then sometimes back.

I'd do it again, go out on that boat
with the urn in one arm, carnations in the other,
spindrift against my face and everything
riding on the changing tide.

Who knows when a hard time will come
or a light shine to cut the darkness?

Who knows when someone will say *No comment*
looking directly at you, making you feel
as unfathomable as you've ever felt.

My 90-Year-Old Mother Would
Be an Alpinist

She's climbing my high porch stairs
pulling herself up by the railing,
her purse slung at her elbow.

She's taking one tread at a time
with an eye on where it matters.

"Jungfrau," she says, without stopping
to take a rest, "Kilimanjaro."

I hear her humming a song she's known
from childhood, little marionettes
about to dance, bowing and curtseying
at the edge of a precipice.

Nothing will ever replace
the magnolia that shades the porch,
that half shades her now in its greenness.

I've offered her my arm
but she loves saying the name
of each difficult mountain,
feeling the slant.

There is no moment that holds her
as well as this one, the body rising
from the shadow-body behind it.

"Mont Blanc," she says, "Aconcagua,"
lifting herself one tread at a time.

Let the mountain monasteries far off
sound their bells, the alpenglow
shine in the distance like stained glass.

Here, too, where steepness is a stairway
leading only to my front door,
every breath is hard won and holy,
every step, a kind of prayer.

What Is a Cat But a Voice Among
All the Other Voices

with apologies to Jeoffrey

She comes to me gleefully when I whistle
for she loves the poetry of sound,
rubbing against my calf, joining in
with a hosanna of caterwauls.

Her name is Thelma, and I will consider her
as lovingly as anyone, for she is a cat as observant
as Christopher Smart's. She meows.
She speaks her mind with ardor
but without violence, forgoing tooth and claw,
gentle among vigorous children.

For she will leap onto the living room table
flitting her tail as an exclamation point,
she will rejoice with song in any empty box,
the last word always hers.

She is a Homer who doesn't nod,
a novelist with an exigent disposition
who stops to neither put a comma in,
nor take it out.

Here she is mewing her way
into the kitchen, looking for praise
and small refrigerated enchantments.

I run my hand along her back
trying to remember the animality of my own skin,
the trees in the slanting light,
the blue sky breathing its blue
down to the greening fields.

Wasn't it wonderful?
Wasn't it momentary to lick the earth
off the body, then put it back again?

She is more cat than dog, more dog
than bird though her face is owl-like,
large-eyed, more fox than owl
when she slithers low.

Now she's on the couch next to me
and what does it mean to be this close
and this far apart, this everything
of being alive together?

She discourses. She sings.
There's no one else who'll know
that my fingers are scratching her head,
that her chin is on my knee,
that our conversations, no matter
how small and local, are worth having.

II

Surprises

My wife says a D# in the key of C
is such a surprise to her ear
it's no wonder people sing in the choir
or play the banjo at odd hours.

Last night, the Algerian delivering our pizza
suddenly broke into French as if we were natives,
invited us to dinner, meet the family,
dip our bread with him in the *tajine*.

Sometimes it's the sound of a rotary phone,
sometimes the clink of milk bottles on the porch.

And here's the elevator man in his uniform
asking us what floor, please, and I'm thinking
how about all of them just for the ride.

Or, maybe, I'd like a slow stairway to heaven,
just to that beach on Planet X
where all my comic book heroes
are lounging about in their swimsuits,
sipping margaritas under a double sun.

Surprises arriving from the recent future.
Or retrieved from the great
irreducible bin of the lost and found.

But now I see my wife wearing
her necklace of silver beads
and almost nothing else, what a surprise!

Oh, the present is unpredictable, too,
appearing sometimes in a blare of trumpets
or as a soft buzz tickling the ear.

Which brings me back to that D#
I'm actually playing now on the guitar

in a song about "Diddy-wah-diddy"
and that great big mystery of love
and sex and the life we try to unravel.

Did I mention I'm taking lessons?
Did I say I'm hitting that D#
as often as I can?

During Our Conversation I'd Like
To Interrupt To Say

Don't be alarmed by the knife
I'm holding against my throat.

It's just my way of saying
how painfully informative you've been
about the pilling on your cardigan sweater,
your ruined umbrella, the tiny drips
falling from your kitchen faucet.

Please, no more "vivid" accounts of your dog
taking a bath, or your mother giving *you* one long ago
which has kept you psychoanalyzed for years,
the stinging soap in your eyes,
the water pot tilting above your head.

Here are some darts to sling at the armoire.
Here is a pair of scissors to mangle a blouse
into little overtures of anger, quick and decisive.

Oh, forgive me if I'm trying too hard
to piece the world back together again
into a smooth, impossible egg
next to the frying pan.

Let's begin by saying something unimaginable:
this torch I'm holding toward you,
light it with your one burnt match.

See? Here's a labyrinth,
here's some thread and only one way
leading to the gist of things,
so many dark passageways
to keep us either hopeful
or tingling with terror.

We can enter it like a conversation
we've always dreamed of having
without scissors or knives.

Whatever we say to each other now
might have every risk of ending badly,
or changing our lives.

Poem with Clouds

After his wife mentioned in passing
that what they were really feeling
each time they kissed
were *her* electrons, *his* electrons,
repulsing each other without touching,

he began kissing everything,
the rough bark of a tree
the cat's furry back,
the piano keys, always smooth.

He wanted to see why one cloud
of electrons was mystifyingly different
from another, why he could distinguish
just by kissing, a potato from a peach pit.

People were beginning to avoid him,
his dogged investigations,
his walk down the street that took hours.

A couple mentioned the Oort Cloud
9 trillion miles away, kiss that
they said, laughing, their arms around each other.

After a while, his lips grew inflamed
as if there were no distance between them
and everything he loved.

One day, a tree fell and he heard it.
Then, he kicked at a rock and it hurt.

He went back to his wife
and gave her a kiss everywhere,

giving her pleasure without ever thinking
of how he was doing it

only that it felt right to do it
which was all they both ever wanted.

And Another Thing

Such dislike for the woman who's come late
to the concert making our whole row rise just
as the tenor sax hits its high E-flat and now
she's sitting next to me and texting—my god!—
during the drummer's lithe percussive
rhythms which are not my rhythms judging
by my heavy foot beats and my fingers
bending into little arcs of stone and I'm thinking
of some way to annihilate her phone invisibly
maybe with a squint of my eye and how lovely
to imagine the stark O of her mouth
her pretty hands holding nothing but the air
I allow her to breathe O most merciful zapper
that I've become father-confessor for all her sins
committed impending unthought-of
her stubborn knees bent to the spectacle
of my very unblind justice which I'd like to take
on tour now and then accosting scofflaws
speedsters unholy maître d's smug
people of all sorts and let's not forget
the dry cleaner who's ruined my favorite shirt
through some occult chemical mishap
and of course this woman sitting next to me
whose soft knit-covered ribs I'm trying hard
not to jab my elbow into but she's smiling now
as if she'd rather be here than anywhere else
riffing with the pianist moving her hips in time

and ok, maybe her lateness wasn't her fault
maybe her husband needed a significant operation
maybe it was poor Aunt Lavinia texting her
that the vicious dog she heard at the door
was really "my own little Shnoozy,"
and shouldn't I maybe introduce myself to her
say what a grand concert this has been judging

from the thunderous standing ovation
everyone's giving the band including me

though didn't the set list seem so short
did they at least play "Splenectomy Blues"
or "Dry Bone Breakdown" and why are we
all filing out when there's so much more
to be mulled over like an old song of the heart
you've carried with you a long time
but can barely hear above all the noise.

Let's Put an End to Grace

I mean the woman who lives next door
with the scowling face and gruesome dog,
the one who won't give back
the kids' balloons that float to her yard.

Put an end. Maybe overly terminal,
poor woman who lavishes
in everyone's ill wishes.

But let's say there were no Grace
to keep our forbearance razor-sharp.
What would that do to the notion
of grace itself if nothing called for it,
every uncivil act requited,
every cruelty blood-let?

The world often bites back
honing its teeth in secret.
And here is Grace herself, holding on
to her iron fence with both hands,
staring fiercely at the empty street
as if nothing can change it.

Sometimes, it's all one gets,
the rubble, the dirt between the toes,
a few tattered feathers.

Then, sometimes, there's nothing better
than hope putting on a silken dress,
walking beyond the edge of town.

Tomorrow, I'll pass by her house
maybe wanting to say, Grace,
thank you for making me think
I'm better than I am

though all I might do, feeling
as inconsequential as rain on lake water,
is say her name again and again

as if I were mouthing an old prayer
full of rags, or expecting an answer.

Nostalgia

My days are billowing backward
like smoke from a ship's funnel
and, frankly, I'm in no rush
for anyone to reach port.

Nostalgia! Isn't it a flaw in every traveler
who stares too longingly at his wake,
though the word, from the Greek *nostos*,
suggests a desire to return home?

I'm caught in some time warp
not knowing where my life's fiesta is,
here in my kitchen, or someplace I've passed through,
Paris, or Altoona maybe, or the Straits
of Messina where I've never been.

I'd like to mention that there are green apples
in my fruit bowl next to the radio.
I like the curlicue peels I can make,
I like the tenor madness that coils
from the speakers into my ear.

My friend says it's a prime Odyssean misadventure,
how we might languish on some uncharted isle
if we lose sight of our past affections.

Though didn't Lot's wife turn back
for that last, lingering look, scattering herself
into ten-thousand selves?

Those apples in my bowl
are giving off a sweet luscious scent
and the music is creating a yearning in me
for more new riffs and *ka-chings*,
and if I had a photograph of every second

of the life I've already lived
I might feel bedraggled by it.

Or maybe not, maybe I'd pore over every snapshot,
nuance, every shade of gray, committing them
to memory, that dear crazy custodian
of all our lunacies and pleasures.

Now the radio's playing "Teenager in Love,"
and that's me! I hear myself saying,
thinking of a Friday night dance
and my first awkward kiss with a girl
that traveled through my heart.

And this is me, too, now with an apple-y succulence
against my mouth, tasting the poignancy
of not being what I was but still beguiled
by this sticky, bewildering
kiss of time on my lips

hearing the young gauzy voices
singing *Why must I be . . .* the past
coursing into the present, the *then*
and the *there* into the here I am.

Loose Ends

I've been pacing the afternoon
like a high-wire walker
from room to room
counting the steps.

Dear Flying Wallendas,
help me reach out across the canyon
of lost connections.
Philippe Petit, speak to me
as if I were your balancing pole.

The letters I've written—
let them send me back a sign
they've been thumbed.
Let the numbers I've called
redial themselves till sunup.

It's the neighbor's pickup driving away
pinging gravel with its tires,
it's the geese barking the end of summer
that's got me wishing for binoculars.

The fall leaves are floating down,
as if they had something important
to say to the ground.

It's been Sunday here all week.
I'm holding out for big box deliveries.
I'm waiting in my soft-soled shoes
for the dog to bark.

Someone, come knock on my door.
Let's see who's inside.

Lies

It's a kindness, sometimes,
how you'd like to say one thing
but choose another, that "luscious roast,"
for instance, you could wear home as a shoe,
the "lovely dress" that reminds you
of a tent flap in a storm.

Yes, you say, it's a dazzling page-turner,
thinking where did the language go to die?

Such are the diplomatic swerves
one takes for friends and family, not to mention
one's beloved, and how lovely to offer them
a dollop of cream instead of the gall.

Of course, some lies are better left unsaid,
their footings crumbling to powder
even before the house is built

but some are so artfully conceived
you almost wish you were the object
of their attentions, *many thanks
for your intricate efforts!*

The world is your oyster your fortune says
with a sleight and a wink
and even *you* seem willing to be huckstered in,
looking for the sweetness in the salt,
and maybe the hidden pearl.

And isn't it too easy to admire the truth
stretching always like a clear expanse
without obstruction or change?

Nothing in its field to cast a shadow
or bend the light in a hundred ways.

Nothing of the lie circling toward you now
with a straight face and the faintest smile
as if to say here is the world, truth be told,
and here it is again, all tangle and curve.

III

Sometimes

Sometimes it doesn't matter what you say,
        sometimes it matters where you are,
under the magnolia tree, for instance,
    the pink blossoms
        looking like giant startled eyes

and somehow there's no need for saying
        anything about the pleasure you feel
    hearing the sound of rain on a barn roof
        or a jazzy minor 7th lifting softly from a piano.

And what is it about holding the hand
        of your best girl and feeling at 14
    nothing of the past or future
just the desire of a boy
        who's lost all his marbles
somewhere between a touch and a kiss?

Sometimes the language of pleasure
        needs no syntax or parsing
    to make you feel everything's in sync.

And here is the crepuscular night
        making you want to connect all the stars
    with your finger in one continuous line
as if you could do it and whatever seems
        furthest from you is nearest.

Sometimes it's how a moment pans out
        into gold maybe, a small shining to hold
    in your hand for luck or mystery.
Sometimes even nothing you can say
        will keep it there.

Bats

They are like the body unhinged
　　the soul made almost visible
　　　　a swerving of wings
　　erratic slicings
that keep us awake
　　　　like narratives that have
no certain end or wavering
　　hands in the fog
　　　　nothing distinct except
their curve and flit
　　　　under sky or bough
　　unbird-like as they are
　　　　　unknotting the air
　　with loops and veers
　　　　catching our blithe attention
　　　　　what makes them suddenly
　　leathery and fearsome
passing as they sometimes do
　　into our lives
　　　　through the smallest apertures
　　we who are their kin
backboned cochlear
　　crouching below them
with our gloves and nets
　　plastic bowls and cookie sheets
all the domesticity we can muster
　　wishing only that the moonlight
　　　might lure them back
　　into a steeper darkness
toward everything they are
　　nocturnal unfeathery
　　silhouettes of incongruous motion
momentary arrhythmic glimpses
　　we endure
　　　keeping our distance.

Beauty

In the eye of the beholder, we say, disregarding
what the beautiful might spring from,
an oil slick's satiny iridescence, the ravishing
splash of orange in the smog-ridden sky.

Yesterday, someone pointed to the loosestrife
overtaking our garden, praised the lovely
delicate petals, the long magisterial stalks.

Sometimes the beautiful is a fire
that takes the whole of a tree in its arms,
sometimes a wild and engorged river
cutting deeply into the land.

The beautiful floats beyond us
immune to our beholding.

Once, on a slow train home
it was the hundred refinery towers
looming eerily over our passage,
flaring like dark angels.

Sometimes it touches us
without scruple or intention,
this arrow's fletching
against my fingers, the soft art
required to bring down, make war.

Sometimes it's almost nothing at all,
a long whistle in the distance,
a startle of new rain,
a woman's delicate hand appearing
in a window, then disappearing
before any implication.

Body to Body

I see my wife sitting among cows
in the far pasture extending her hand
toward the closest ones, their soft lips
nuzzling against her palm, an understanding
between two skins, a gentleness requited,
and others grazing now around her as though
they were saying something quiet
with their bodies and she to them,
her knee bandaged from a torn ligament,
her one eye darkening too soon
and body to body they seem without thought
lifting from out of each other
the pleasure of being elsewise and together
and I remember the hummingbird she once held
delicately by its feet becoming part of her hand
before it thrummed to the topmost branches
or the gopher snake that coiled around her arm
making it more lively than any other
or the time she stood in the lake
and kissed my mouth and made me
hunger for water, fishing water,
rowing water, water cascading
down my body in rivulets
and there she is among cows
hearing their grunts and chuffs
being their companion
without forwardness or guile,
pleasure neither exceeding
the moment nor a moment's
pleasure, that twining
that sufficient touch
of the touch.

Startled from Sleep

Something shakes me from my sleep
making me walk from room to room
as if I were finding a way to return
as if looking out windows opening the door
breathing the darkness into my body
would make me less provisory
as I had been in my dream
without any words of my own
hearing only the distant songs
others were singing. Something.

Undoing Song

Let a clear sky reel around a greening field
And the field unfurl its tall white pines.
And the pitched ax lay them side by side
Into the hewn shape of a house.

Let the house find shelter by a lofty oak
And the acorns drop through the leaves like rain.
Let the rain abound to slake the throat
Of a thirsty mouse who finds harbor there.

Then let the night cat take the mouse
And the fox slit the cat in a glint of hunger
And the hunter bring down the satiny fox
And a wayward scythe untether the man.

Let the earth unleash its volcanic clouds
Unmetaling every scythe in its spew,
And death itself undo itself
With nothing to cleave its nothing to.

When It Is Time

When it is time that my heart begins
to dance the *fado* even before I hear its music
I can feel the animals shepherding themselves
away from the shallow face of the earth
into a deeper sleep the wasps combing
the creviced side of the house every spider
along the eaves casting its delicate web
against the soon-to-be and how many times
have I watched in a riot of color things
that have disappeared not to return again
until another spring not knowing
how many among them might remember
this day when I felt in the silence
of my own astonishment
their fugitive presences.

Homecoming

There's a heavy knocking on your door
and suddenly the door seems incidental.
Take the rugs, you say,
take the food, but they take you.

Say you're only imagining it,
but what if you disappear for years
sitting in your own parlor
without anyone calling your name?

Every morning, you feed the cat,
make the coffee, invite the news
to join you for a cup, flood-tides,
fire-gusts, the crowded Kuiper Belt.

Even the small upheavals now
are as noticeable to you
as the larger ones, the carpenter bees
poking holes in your walls.

You'd like the future to stay where it is
blighting someone else's garden
or rising with the smoke
above a city you've never been to.

Isn't it ingenious being alive
as if you've had some say in it?
There's nothing to do but believe
you'll be right where you are

until the cows come home.
Which they do. Every day,
as any farmer will tell you.
Look there, across the fields.

Stuff

I'm packing up my son's toy trumpet,
the one with a missing valve.
I'm storing my grandmother's wool coat
in a box among all the other boxes.

Serving plates, eyeglasses, books,
old letters in a fine hand—
so much stuff has collected,
bags of it, suitcases.

I'd like to know what Einstein kept in his satchel
when he left Zurich forever,
what Rosa Bonheur tossed out
to make her workroom roomier.

At night, I imagine the sheep I count
are flocking in my basement.
In the morning, I find two of everything,
sugar bowls, newspapers, coffee urns.

Somewhere, milkweed pods
must be blowing away like froth,
a kite is snipping its own taut string.

I look at my grandfather's nightshirts
hanging disconsolately in my closet,
my father's thumbprints
are on the accordion I never play.

Generations unraveling—how many?
before the memory of the person is lost,
photographs of faces that have no names,
billet-doux that leave no addresses?

Stuff of our days prolonging us.

That pewter mug out of which he drank.
The letter she wrote one morning
as the fog lifted off the ocean
and she thought of a flute playing.

All Those Whom I Have Loved

How often have I stood in a field
practicing for their departures
all those whom I have loved
and who have loved back
until I am bereft and speechless
thinking *this is how it will be one day*
the morning fog lifting from the hollows
and nothing of this field remaining
not even what has held me here
shamelessly and without reason
at the edge of my small poignancies
as if they were what mattered
as if they were the grief
that will come one day
as it will.

Other Lessons

The guitar neck is fretted with so many notes
I've lost my way among the G#s and flats
the major 7ths, all the diminished chords.

That's how I'm feeling, shrunken
smaller than a pinhole.

Someone must be playing now
in a smoky bar with the ghost
of Big Bill Broonzy at his shoulder
hearing the music of his name
hum in his body.

I should play by ear someone tells me
but I can't hear where the rain
is falling now, how many birds
are alighting on the branches.

Sometimes it's just better to listen
before you can do something about it.

There's rosewood in my arms
the guitar strings are glittering
like moonlight on water.

Something far away
is moving through a dark forest
drinking from a river
without making a sound.

IV

A Moment Without Objects

Suddenly I felt something had been forgotten
and I went from cupboard to bed stand
to coffee mug and desk to find what I thought

had been missing from my life
as though I could find it
where I had spent most of my hours.

I sharpened a pencil, I plucked
a guitar string, though nothing seemed to be
different from what had always been.

I said *mountain* then *desert*
as if the two contrarieties
would offer me a doorway
to a sideways landscape

though everything stood as it was
while I counted my breaths
without keeping track of the number.

Then there was a shrill sound
outside, a blue jay's screech,
a shadow of wing tipping the balance.

Then the noise of the house readjusting its planks
and sunlight falling on the kitchen floor
and my fingers running slowly
along the smooth apparition of morning
without knowing why.

Even During the Slightest Changes

for James Tate, d. July 8, 2015

Everything is in flux, Heraclitus said,
and I believe him with my ragged heart.

My father in his boat
must be rowing on an ancient river
that might be a river
I will never touch.

My mother is standing on a station platform
gathering up her skirts
against the onrushing trains
that are neither arriving nor departing.

Whoever said life is a fire
we're ravished by
must never have been burned
a thousand times.

Tonight, my cousin's tumor
is drumming too loudly in her brain,
making her listen with a different ear.

*The challenge of poetry is to find
the ultimate in ordinary horseshit*
James Tate said, who is now
one among all the mysterious others,
his body at the last unwritten.

Tomorrow, when I wake,
I will think of the weather as I always do,
how I ask after it each day
with the same implacable question,
how, even during the slightest changes,
it is altogether different.

Episode at the Neighbors' House

It wasn't the food or company,
we were laughing, everything
had an aromatic shape to it,
the wine, the rich sauces,
the jazz that reminded us
of late hours and smoke.

It wasn't the good talk, politics,
religion, delicious gossip,
all we wanted to say to each other
without anyone coming undone.

It was as if something were eluding us
even as the night got darker
and the darkness painted the windows
a color we could almost touch.

Maybe it had something to do
with the sound of the wind
rushing through the garden
or the garden itself releasing
its hundred petals.

It wasn't love or friendship,
it was a small disturbance,
longing one of us said
though that wasn't exactly it.

It was something like a hollow
in the throat, a hole
inside the hole of the eye

a stone shining in a river
that made the river seem emptier.

What I Was Thinking of During the Funeral Service, Douglas, Arizona

for Wendy Glenn

Of course, death, how it wore
its outsize black hat to slice the day.

The mysterious abyss
of the body failing again,
falling into another body.

Not so much of resurrection
though it was spoken of, the oxen kneeling
in the straw, the stone rolled away.

The first death that had no likeness.
The earth that hath opened her mouth
to receive thy brother's blood.
After which the history of departures
required a history of common prayer.

The husband, the daughter, the long river
they would soon be walking beside.

All the pressed white shirts, the cowhide boots
and blue jeans, the colors of mourning.
Amazing grace. Most merciful Father.

So many words delivered to replace
the touch of the body,
here, touch *wife*, touch *mother.*

Every noise the emblem of something
in motion. The ceiling fans whirring.
The tick, tick, tick, of the sun
beating down on the metal roof.

Just the Facts

We were lying near the ocean
under the thousand stars
we could see pinning
the darkness to the darkness.

It was hard to imagine the emptiness
between one star and another, the distances
requiring us to add so many zeroes.

At every second, a trillion
neutrinos were streaming through our bodies
without hitting anything we were made of.

All this time we'd been asking ourselves
why it mattered, why we put one number
next to another, one color, one heart
holding on to the next.

There was a spit of land we could see
jutting out into the ocean
where the water had thrown itself up for years
against something rockier than itself
and there'd been no winners.

The waves were curling around our ankles
as we walked toward it,
making our footsteps disappear.

If anyone had asked us
what we were holding
we would have said *hands*,

something almost simple like that
and now, more than ever, explicable.

Change

Whatever he did today, it wasn't enough.
That's what he was thinking as he walked down
the street of boutiques and coffee bars,
feeling a little smug that he was passing up both.

The true measure of an act of kindness
he remembered someone saying
is how inconvenient it is for the doer.

He had often given money,
a little of his time, but the world
was still what it was, its indecencies
piling up like gold coins in a vault
and every tyrant in his imagination
smiling broadly from all the screens.

How often, he was ashamed to say,
he had wished for the angel of death
to visit with her sword of a thousand cuts
to do unto others without mercy.

There were words he wished he could whisper to iron
to change the hardest substance of things,
incantations to spill over water
that had the sound of solace and balm.

Had his life come to this, a stroll
through easy neighborhoods and small decisions
as if he could choose *either/or* with little consequence?

He wanted superpowers.
He wanted to feel a flashy superhero suit
under his loose shirt and jeans
rubbing against his muscles.
He wanted his fist to be all fist.

Blessed were those, he knew,
who had been broken and refused
to take up the lash, blessed
the hands that were equal to the flesh.

But there was his prim house again,
and his front door, and a stranger
walking up the porch stairs
he either had to say hello to
or walk away from,

someone who might be the angel of death
or the angel of everything merciful,
depending on what he decided.

Why I'm Not in Cairo (Care-o), Illinois,
Honking My Horn Like a Happy Tourist

Because I live in Philadelphia, PA,
  which also sits between two rivers.
Because I was born near Cairo, Egypt,
  and have eaten of its grilled corn and pigeon.
Because I don't know how to say Care-o and mean it.
Because I have no great-aunts to pull me forth,
  no uncles who have lain under its fields.
Because Little Egypt for me has always been a belly dancer
  jouncing my imagination.
Because the confluence of the Mississippi and Ohio
  should be great unto itself without the specter of the Nile
  breathing above its waters.
Because there are so many other rare convergences,
  Yassou! Athens, Ohio. Paris, Texas, *je t'embrasse.*
Because I love how Robert Bly has written of Minnesota,
  "the soybeans are breathing on all sides,"
  and how could they be breathing likewise in southern Illinois?
Because there is a cloud over the half-empty streets
  and shuttered grocery stores.
Because *Life on the Mississippi*, Part 1,
  is an elegiac praise of a river
  on the verge of changing utterly.
Because the history of Cairo includes its own chronicle
  of violence and a failure of the heart
  that is not unusual.
Because I've run out of pushpins and maps.
Because I dream of someone standing on a highway
  holding up a hand, saying, *end of the line.*
Because there is not an adequate way of seeing the world
  in one small lifetime and a hundred promises.
Because every difficult place has its own encounters.
Because all the roads lead home.

Traveling into Deeper Country

Cochise County, AZ

It was the year the swallows nested in the eaves
making a racket, the year the gopher snake
glided up the tree straight as a rod.

There was no guessing what we'd see next,
scorpions under a black light,
javelinas clattering on the front porch.

The city seemed like a sepia photograph
we'd left behind, the drizzly streets full of traffic,
the subway vents ghosting their plumes of steam.

It was monsoon season, season of promise
for the high desert ranches, dust-ridden
and parched through the year-long drought
and every foreclosure sign we passed
along abandoned fields and homesteads
made us think twice of our romance
with wide open spaces, fences unraveled,
doors hammered shut.

Nights were onyx black, star-stunned
in a way that made the darkness
almost companionable.

The day before, we'd found a migrant woman
lying half-conscious by the Pedregosa foothills,
eyes glazed, body unable to take water,
and soon, the ambulance we'd called for
carted her away to who knows where
and we wondered what kind of life
we were supposed to live.

Sometimes we drew our blinds against the dark.
Sometimes we thought we heard gunshots,
or was it thunder, or the sonic booms from F–16s
training along the borderland,
jolting us to alertness.

There was nothing to do but breathe in the wind.
It was a matter of keeping still,
watching rain clouds drifting over the Chiricahuas
hoping they'd veer our way, a matter of
walking through the tall brown grass
thinking greenness was an extravagance
we remembered touching.

We were looking at the horses in the neighboring fields
suddenly galloping together, delirious,
raising great sheaves of dust.

We were looking at the full moon rising
between the mountains, and the sun
flaring just above the opposite horizon.

We were tourists in a land that took our breath away.
How could we ever live
among this stark communion of things,
and how could we not?

We were sitting on the porch
trying to identify the many birds
that flashed their iridescent colors
and we were wondering about the mountain lion
someone had seen prowling in the far fields,
the half-gnawed deer it had buried
for another reaping.

Now two strangers were coming up the road,
worn, as if they'd crossed over the mountains,
calling out, *We mean no harm,*
wanting only to find the apple orchards
where there was work.

Something for the journey, we said,
and watched them walk away with food and water
into the almost dark where people
kept appearing and disappearing
and the beautiful and raw
took turns mounting their spectacles.

It was night and the stars began to emerge
one by one as if they had waited all year
to show themselves, and the desert voices
began to carry toward us unobstructed.

We walked out into the darkness
to feel it better, hardly seeing
where we were stepping, everything
depending now on what we knew
or thought we knew—or what
we were willing to risk.

V

My Mother Considers Her Death During Cocktail Hour

It will be a sleep without dreams, she thinks.
Or someone ushering her into a plush limo.

No other alternatives for her,
though she'd like the limo
to carry a full bar.

Nothing about becoming pure light
or hearing a birdsong at the edge of a field
and wanting to *be* the song.

"I'd rather hear something heftier," she says,
"a coffee grinder, a deep-muscle massager,
something to keep me rolling."

She's stopped waiting for her father
to unhook the swinging door.
The sound of wind in the chimney
has been nothing but wind.

"My turn," she says, "all the lights are green,
I'm almost at the exit ramp."

Outside, the cumulus clouds
are silently scudding away from all the ruckus,
geese are writing the sky
with invisible quills.

Tomorrow, she might recite the poems
she's loved, haply remembering
the violins of autumn that wound the heart
and evening slowly latching the garden gates.

But now, she's after a dollop of bourbon,
it's cocktail time, we're clinking to the great beyond—
stars, galaxies, rocketing our imagination
toward what may last or fall—

and here's to the sheer improbability
of being where we are, making
a small place in the world
where a history of our loves and losses
shapes us into who we are.

"Here's to forgetfulness, too," she says,
turning on the lights, "give me an absence
that stays absent without any trouble."

Sometimes, there's nothing the world can add
to make itself more than it is.

Outside, we hear the wind howling
in joy or anger, what a mystery
we make of it, and looking out
onto the steepest darkness, our lit windows
are like large unblinking eyes.

Ghost Dog

I dream she comes to me when it's cold
and the windows are ice-crackled and hard
and she snuffles at the linen sheets
and licks the bedposts for the salt.

I can almost smell the odor of wet fur,
feel her breath along my fingertips.

But she must be a shadow now in the moonlit field
or traveling an unwinding road
and all the rivers are one river for her,
and all the woods without demarcation.

Still, I've put out paper lanterns
by the roadside, whispered her name
into the bordering trees.

Is there ever a goodbye that echoes back an answer?
I stand at the window tracing a line of ice
as if it were a frozen river
anyone might cross.

Goodnight, old ghost. Goodnight
to all that isn't here. And all that is.

In every bark I hear, I hear her bark.
In every gust of wind, the sound
of something passing on its way,
unleashed and masterless.

Horse Heaven

One day I will cross this road
into the neighbor's field for the last time
and wade into the high grass
as I would into water

And I will see a horse I have never seen
standing easily in the greenness of the world
without effort or impatience
its warm nuzzling mouth
the delicate pastern and hock
being the indelible signs of its likeness

And I will think there is nothing but horse
that could carry me to the edge
of everything I have ever known
through any desert or alpine cold
its belly ribbed and hard
its haunches ropes of muscle

And should there be a sudden upthrust of wind
I will whisper to it a prayer of gratitude
for all its watchfulness

And if the rain swells in a heave
stinging my back I will take shelter
under the great vault of its neck

And if anyone should ask
what I would wish for in this field
where no one might ask anything of me again

I will say it is to be surrounded
by the insistent odor of horse
to see its ears tuning themselves to the slightest sound

to feel as it must feel
the grass growing noiselessly
under the four dominions of its hooves.

A Roost of Turkeys

They are dropping down from the apple trees
some twenty of them wild turkeys
in the early morning winging softly to the ground
feathery air-lightened becoming such awkward
trekkers of the earth their vulturey heads
bobbing with each step as if to say *yes yes*
to the copious world omnivores gobbling
salamanders seeds blueberries worms
moving in a line toward tall grass or woods
in whose shelter they'll disappear before
the sun unleashes its depredations hawk's talons
weasel's jaw gunshots spiking the silence
but how heartening to see them now
sojourners of the in-between gravity-bound
bird embodied rising above us only to fall
like ragged angels we meet in our dreams
half hoping they will keep scouring our fields
half hoping they will vault the sky.

An Uneven Dozen

Therefore

The hand at the end of my arm,
how far away it feels
from what I think I am.

A tree must know its branches
as itself, spiraling outward
without losing touch.

Cat kneading my thigh, how quickly
you bring me back to myself,
as if I had strayed away too long
to be of use to the world.

Inexplicable the Heart

Last night, a rare blood moon
reddening the sky above the trees.

Why did I turn and point
to every familiar constellation?

Whatever Else We Are

As with fire, ashes.
As with body, a final spilling
into minutest parts.
As with love, the end
of all our histories.

Whatever It Is

The field covered in translucent fog.
A songbird hidden, singing.
If I could see the field,
if I could track the songbird's flight,
would I be any happier?

Other Ways

Blue larkspur against the barn—
how many times have I looked at it
without noticing a ruby-throated humming
tonguing the nectar.

Transposition

My cat again, perched at the window,
held in thrall by something outside,
though I can see little of what she sees.
Isn't this what we're after,
being in the world
of so many worlds?

Door

It swings easily back and forth,
letting in, letting out.
Even when locked,
it is still a door. But more so.

From One Life into Another

As I walk out to my mailbox
to rummage through the darkness
I see that the phoebe's nest in the low eaves
is empty of its hatchlings.

Somewhere, a letter written in a fine hand
is shining up from a kitchen table, the evening
brims with song and small wingbeats.

That, Too, Is Sufficient

How many years have I lost
thinking of what I should do next
without intending to do it.

The trees move when the wind rises.
Even I will pick up the hammer
when the nail tells me to.

Antinomies

The paradox of time, giving me too much time
and sometimes not enough at the same time.
Morning, evening. Seconds, years.
When I'm late for everything,
I'm early for everything else.

The Way of Things

The apple eaten by the worm.
Rose-leaf undone by the beetle.

Tomorrow, I'll climb the mountain
where I've never been
where the wild lion prowls
and rattlesnakes coil among rocks.

Poor house standing alone in the clearing.

Without Saying

So many goodbyes waiting for me
next month, next year, so many
dangerous curves ahead,
slippery weather.

How to say what I feel
without misplacing the feeling,
the spoken, the unspoken.

Little magical hand
I am attached to,
waving in the rain.

Transmogrification

Sometimes the body is made of rocks,
sometimes of cotton.
In the ice tray, what was once water.
In a diamond, a history of stars.
And we think there is only one shape
identifying us forever.

Reconstitutions, Dispersions

There's an easiness in how the Black River
parts around the rocks
then comes together almost as itself.

Foxes deep among the trees,
beetles underneath the stones,
I'd like to sense them the way bees sense
the ultraviolet shining in flowers
as if they *were* the flowers.

I smell the earth in a handful of earth,
touch the atoms I might one day be colluding with.
I look at honeysuckle and think *goshawk*,
finger a willow branch and say *lodestone*.

Maybe that loose amalgam I've called *ghost*
might reappear one day as a mourning dove
fluttering at night against my window.

I, I, I, (as in *impermeable*):
how much of the elemental world
has seeped into that slender vowel,
and become part of the alphabet of my body.

The cold is pimpling my arms, and maybe
a molecule of me might have been part
of some plump goose a thousand years ago,
the air it breathed what I'm breathing here.

The river I put my hand into now,
river I might become, imagining
the feel of trout gill, fox tongue,
taking me, drinking me in.

Bad News Day in Spring

What a truism to repeat again and again:
we're all slipping away and everyone's on schedule.
It's a bad day to have a body, and a mind
that has no pleasure in thinking about it.

Malignancies, tumors, pearls
of radiation, why not shovel them all
into the firebox of an old locomotive, set the levers
for the Museum of the Never-to-be-Seen-Again.

Outside, the daffodils are showing their skirts,
the snow is unfurling its many scarves
from around the lilacs and fig trees.

If there's a prediction of rain,
let's get out the barrels and collection troughs
and pin our swimsuits on every clothesline.

Isn't it time for a drink at least,
one with a fanciful umbrella in it?

Patches of grass are as green as they've ever been
even before we've thought
of flinging our gloves into the winter basket.

Sometimes the world is out
to get us on its side, without fanfare,
being just what it is

though how many of us might be cooking dinner,
sifting the laundry, receiving a call that changes
the truth of what we are, we who've been
wayfarers of darkness these past months

wanting nothing more than to see
the bare earth against our knees again
and flecks of mica shining back the sun,
or hear the sound of rivers purling
as the ice releases.

What I Want

I'd like to lift a slab of city sidewalk
to rediscover the secret rummaging of wood-lice,
feel the grid-work of tree roots in the underneath.

I'd like to perfect a two-fingered whistle
to call horses and cows to shelter.
And how lovely to be adept
at playing the instrument of one's body.

I want to breathe in light from the furthest star,
weigh an atom of iron on my fingertip.

May the cockeyed angles of my bedroom windows
teach me how to be whimsical without effort.

And here's to my irreverent friend
for wanting to have *Check, please!*
carved on his gravestone.

I want to say the right words
at the right time
especially when I'm in the wrong place.

I can almost hear the cornstalks in my neighbor's field
rustling at night as they grow,
turning greener, leafier.

I want to kneel without having to pray,
to praise without raising a flag of praise.

I want to keep wanting whatever is hard to hold,
seeds in the desert, words floating on water,
faces where there are no faces.

Thankfulness

I'm always swept away by jazz,
the syncopation, the brushes against the skin,
the bass lines running up and down
the fingerboard like water.

Even when I'm writing a letter of condolence,
or a poem of praise, trying to burnish a stubborn turn
of phrase, here comes the thought of a saxophone riff
climbing up my spine like sexy, insistent fingers
I can't resist and don't want to.

I have foundered on the clarinet, the blues guitar,
taken piano lessons for nine remarkably hopeless years
and no one has knocked on my door
yelling *You bet, baby, you're it!*

There are times you hope to be made better
than you are, and sometimes
it happens, the world takes a look at you
and says, you're due.

Then sometimes everything ends up in a laundry chute
or on a city street where no one bothers
to pick anything up.

But here's Coltrane's solo on "My Favorite Things"
which has become one of my favorite things.
Here's Miles trumpeting *so what, so what,*
so saucily it causes a momentary gladness
in me and all that I do.

Sometimes loveliness is other people
pulling you in their wake toward a different island,
the island you've always imagined floating toward
and maybe never reaching,

except for those temporary reprieves
when you're suddenly filled with gratitude
for being where you are, on the same planet
as someone who's just played a genius note
or spoken a word that was never there
until it was.

Previous titles in the Carnegie Mellon Poetry Series

2000
Small Boat with Oars of Different Size, Thom Ward
Post Meridian, Mary Ruefle
Hierarchies of Rue, Roger Sauls
Constant Longing, Dennis Sampson
Mortal Education, Joyce Peseroff
How Things Are, James Richardson
Years Later, Gregory Djanikian
On the Waterbed They Sank to Their Own Levels, Sarah Rosenblatt
Blue Jesus, Jim Daniels
Winter Morning Walks: 100 Postcards to Jim Harrison, Ted Kooser

2001
The Deepest Part of the River, Mekeel McBride
The Origin of Green, T. Alan Broughton
Day Moon, Jon Anderson
Glacier Wine, Maura Stanton
Earthly, Michael McFee
Lovers in the Used World, Gillian Conoley
Sex Lives of the Poor and Obscure, David Schloss
Voyages in English, Dara Wier
Quarters, James Harms
Mastodon, 80% Complete, Jonathan Johnson
Ten Thousand Good Mornings, James Reiss
The World's Last Night, Margot Schilpp

2002
Among the Musk Ox People, Mary Ruefle
The Memphis Letters, Jay Meek
What It Wasn't, Laura Kasischke
The Finger Bone, Kevin Prufer
The Late World, Arthur Smith
Slow Risen Among the Smoke Trees, Elizabeth Kirschner
Keeping Time, Suzanne Cleary
Astronaut, Brian Henry

2003
Trouble, Mary Baine Campbell
A Place Made of Starlight, Peter Cooley
Taking Down the Angel, Jeff Friedman
Lives of Water, John Hoppenthaler
Imitation of Life, Allison Joseph
Except for One Obscene Brushstroke, Dzvinia Orlowsky
The Mastery Impulse, Ricardo Pau-Llosa
Casino of the Sun, Jerry Williams

2004
The Women Who Loved Elvis All Their Lives, Fleda Brown
The Chronic Liar Buys a Canary, Elizabeth Edwards
Freeways and Aqueducts, James Harms
Prague Winter, Richard Katrovas
Trains in Winter, Jay Meek
Tristimania, Mary Ruefle
Venus Examines Her Breast, Maureen Seaton
Various Orbits, Thom Ward

2005
Things I Can't Tell You, Michael Dennis Browne
Bent to the Earth, Blas Manuel De Luna
Blindsight, Carol Hamilton
Fallen from a Chariot, Kevin Prufer
Needlegrass, Dennis Sampson
Laws of My Nature, Margot Schilpp
Sleeping Woman, Herbert Scott
Renovation, Jeffrey Thomson

2006
Burn the Field, Amy Beeder
The Sadness of Others, Hayan Charara
A Grammar to Waking, Nancy Eimers
Dog Star Delicatessen: New and Selected Poems 1979–2006, Mekeel
    McBride
Shinemaster, Michael McFee

Eastern Mountain Time, Joyce Peseroff
Dragging the Lake, Robert Thomas

2007
Trick Pear, Suzanne Cleary
So I Will Till the Ground, Gregory Djanikian
Black Threads, Jeff Friedman
Drift and Pulse, Kathleen Halme
The Playhouse Near Dark, Elizabeth Holmes
On the Vanishing of Large Creatures, Susan Hutton
One Season Behind, Sarah Rosenblatt
Indeed I Was Pleased with the World, Mary Ruefle
The Situation, John Skoyles

2008
The Grace of Necessity, Samuel Green
After West, James Harms
Anticipate the Coming Reservoir, John Hoppenthaler
Convertible Night, Flurry of Stones, Dzvinia Orlowsky
Parable Hunter, Ricardo Pau-Llosa
The Book of Sleep, Eleanor Stanford

2009
Divine Margins, Peter Cooley
Cultural Studies, Kevin A. González
Dear Apocalypse, K. A. Hays
Warhol-o-rama, Peter Oresick
Cave of the Yellow Volkswagen, Maureen Seaton
Group Portrait from Hell, David Schloss
Birdwatching in Wartime, Jeffrey Thomson

2010
The Diminishing House, Nicky Beer
A World Remembered, T. Alan Broughton
Say Sand, Daniel Coudriet
Knock Knock, Heather Hartley
In the Land We Imagined Ourselves, Jonathan Johnson

Selected Early Poems: 1958-1983, Greg Kuzma
The Other Life: Selected Poems, Herbert Scott
Admission, Jerry Williams

2011
Having a Little Talk with Capital P Poetry, Jim Daniels
Oz, Nancy Eimers
Working in Flour, Jeff Friedman
Scorpio Rising: Selected Poems, Richard Katrovas
The Politics, Benjamin Paloff
Copperhead, Rachel Richardson

2012
Now Make an Altar, Amy Beeder
Still Some Cake, James Cummins
Comet Scar, James Harms
Early Creatures, Native Gods, K. A. Hays
That Was Oasis, Michael McFee
Blue Rust, Joseph Millar
Spitshine, Anne Marie Rooney
Civil Twilight, Margot Schilpp

2013
Oregon, Henry Carlile
Selvage, Donna Johnson
At the Autopsy of Vaslav Nijinksy, Bridget Lowe
Silvertone, Dzvinia Orlowsky
Fibonacci Batman: New & Selected Poems (1991-2011), Maureen Seaton
When We Were Cherished, Eve Shelnutt
The Fortunate Era, Arthur Smith
Birds of the Air, David Yezzi

2014
Night Bus to the Afterlife, Peter Cooley
Alexandria, Jasmine Bailey
Dear Gravity, Gregory Djanikian
Pretenders, Jeff Friedman

How I Went Red, Maggie Glover
All That Might Be Done, Samuel Green
Man, Ricardo Pau-Llosa
The Wingless, Cecilia Llompart

2015
The Octopus Game, Nicky Beer
The Voices, Michael Dennis Browne
Domestic Garden, John Hoppenthaler
We Mammals in Hospitable Times, Jynne Dilling Martin
And His Orchestra, Benjamin Paloff
Know Thyself, Joyce Peseroff
cadabra, Dan Rosenberg
The Long Haul, Vern Rutsala
Bartram's Garden, Eleanor Stanford

2016
Something Sinister, Hayan Charara
The Spokes of Venus, Rebecca Morgan Frank
Adult Swim, Heather Hartley
Swastika into Lotus, Richard Katrovas
The Nomenclature of Small Things, Lynn Pedersen
Hundred-Year Wave, Rachel Richardson
Where Are We in This Story, Sarah Rosenblatt
Inside Job, John Skoyles
Suddenly It's Evening: Selected Poems, John Skoyles

2017
Disappeared, Jasmine V. Bailey
Custody of the Eyes, Kimberly Burwick
Dream of the Gone-From City, Barbara Edelman
Sometimes We're All Living in a Foreign Country, Rebecca Morgan Frank
Rowing with Wings, James Harms
Windthrow, K. A. Hays
We Were Once Here, Michael McFee
Kingdom, Joseph Millar
The Histories, Jason Whitmarsh

2018

World Without Finishing, Peter Cooley
May Is an Island, Jonathan Johnson
The End of Spectacle, Virginia Konchan
Big Windows, Lauren Moseley
Bad Harvest, Dzvinia Orlowsky
The Turning, Ricardo Pau-Llosa
Immortal Village, Kathryn Rhett
No Beautiful, Anne Marie Rooney
Last City, Brian Sneeden
Imaginal Marriage, Eleanor Stanford
Black Sea, David Yezzi

2019

The Complaints, W. S. Di Piero
Brightword, Kimberly Burwick
Ordinary Chaos, Kimberly Kruge
Mad Tiny, Emily Pettit
Afterswarm, Margot Schilpp

2020

Sojourners of the In-Between, Gregory Djanikian
Any God Will Do, Virginia Konchan
My Second Work, Bridget Lowe
Flourish, Dora Malech
Take Nothing, Deborah Pope